Bears

D0460578

Einstein Sisters

KidsWorld

About

Bears are found in North and South America, Europe and Asia. There are **no bears** native to Africa, Australia or Antarctica.

Bears

Most bears have a **large,** stocky body, short legs and a **long snout.**

Bears are good swimmers. Some are also very good **at climbing trees.**

Bears eat
many different things.
They like grass, berries
and nuts. They also eat bees,
ants and termites, small animals
like mice and squirrels, fish
and dead animals. They
eat garbage, too.

Bears have a really good **sense of smell.**

Bears can **stand up** on their hind feet. They do this when they want to **look around** or smell something.

Bears can **see things** that are far away. They **can't see** very well **up close.**

The only
bears that **hibernate**
are **black bears** and **brown
bears**. Polar bears are **active
all year** round. Bears that
live in **warm** parts of the
world don't need to sleep
during the winter.

Some bears **hibernate.** That means they sleep for most **of the winter.**

Bears don't eat, drink or poop while they are **hibernating.**

Bears **hibernate** in dens. A **den** can be a small cave, a hole in tree or a **nest** on the **ground.**

Hibernation

Newborn cubs are very small. They have **almost no fur** and are blind and **helpless.**

Cubs

A female bear usually has **one to three cubs.** The cubs are born in winter. They **stay in the den** with their mother until **spring.**

A **baby bear** is called **a cub.**

Cubs weigh about **500 grams** when they are born. That's about the same as **half a loaf of bread.**

A mother bear is **very dangerous** when she is **protecting** her cubs. **Never go close** to a bear cub in the **wild**.

Bear cubs like to **play**. Play fighting **makes the cubs strong** and teaches them to **protect** themselves.

The cubs usually **stay** with **their mother** for up to **two years**.

Cubs follow their mother. She **teaches them** to find food and to hunt.

Black Bear

The American black bear has a **large body** covered with **thick fur**. It has a **short tail**, small eyes, rounded ears and a long snout.

These **bears** only live in **Canada**, the United States and Mexico.

Black bears usually live in forests. They are also found in mountains and **swamps.**

The bear's thick, **shaggy fur** keeps it warm in **the winter.**

Black bears have **short claws** so they can **climb trees.**

Not all black bears are **black.** They can also be very dark brown, **cinnamon-coloured** and even **pure white.**

Black bears can live for **more** than 25 years.

Black bears look **clumsy** but they can **run very fast.** They are also very good swimmers.

Bears are **very strong** and **unpredictable. Always** treat them with caution and respect.

Black bears eat roots, berries, meat, fish, bugs and plants. They sometimes **hunt** young deer and moose. They also like honey.

The Kermode bear is sometimes called the **"spirit bear."** It is important in First Nations culture.

This bear is named after **Francis Kermode,** a **zoologist** at the Royal British Columbia **Museum.**

The Kermode bear is a kind of black bear, but **it is white.** Even its **claws** are white. It is not related to the polar bear.

Kermode Bear

Kermode bears eat all kinds of plants, fruit, insects, nuts, salmon, mice and **squirrels.**

This bear **lives only in Canada.** It is found in **rainforests** in **coastal** areas of British Columbia.

This bear is the **official animal of British Columbia.**

Brown bears have a **hump** between their shoulders. The American black bear does not, so the hump is a good way to tell the two kinds of bears **apart.**

The brown bear is found in forests and mountains in North America, Europe and Asia. It is the most common kind of bear in the world.

Brown

An adult brown bear weighs more than a piano.

Bear

A brown bear's claws can be as **long** as adult human fingers. The bear uses its claws to dig up plant roots and to make its den.

Brown bear cubs can climb trees, but adult bears can't.

Brown bears can hear and smell really well, but they have poor eyesight.

The largest brown bears live in **Alaska** and eastern **Russia**.

Brown bears are **very good** swimmers.

They eat **mostly** berries, nuts, grass, roots, honey, insects, birds and fish. They **also eat** mice, squirrels and young **moose or deer.**

During fall, brown bears **eat almost all day.** They have to **fatten** up before they **hibernate.**

Grizzly Bear

Grizzly bears have **brown fur**, but the hairs on their back and shoulders have **white tips**. That gives the bears a "grizzled" look, which is how they got their name.

Grizzly bears are **good swimmers**. They can also run really **fast**.

The **grizzly bear** is a kind of brown bear. **It lives in** western **Canada** and the northwestern United States.

Grizzly bears eat nuts, berries, leaves, and roots. Sometimes they eat **mice and squirrels** and young moose or deer. They really **love salmon!**

Grizzly bears scratch their backs on trees. They leave their smell and hair on the trees to **mark their territory.**

Grizzly bears are very smart. They also have **good memories.**

Grizzlies can mate with polar bears. The result is called a **"grolar"** or **"pizzly."**

Polar Bear

The polar bear is the **biggest** member of the bear family.

Polar bears live in the Arctic. They are found in Canada, the United States (in Alaska), Russia, Greenland and Norway.

The **polar bear's** small, round ears and short tail help its body conserve heat.

Rough footpads and **sharp claws** help the polar bear **walk on ice.**

The only parts of the bear's body that **don't have fur** are its **footpads** and the **tip of its nose.**

Nearly two-thirds of the **world's** polar bears live in **Canada.** They spend most of their time on Arctic sea ice.

Thick fur and a layer of **fat** keep the bear warm. Under their fur, **polar bears** have **black skin.** Their dark skin absorbs heat from the **sun's rays.**

Females dig dens in deep **snowdrifts. They give** birth in winter, usually to twins.

Polar bears are **strong swimmers.** Their large, flat front feet help them **move** through the water. They sometimes hunt by swimming **under** the ice.

Polar bears eat mostly seals. They often sit at a seal's **breathing hole** in the ice and **wait** for the seal to come up from the water.

Spectacled Bear

The spectacled bear is one of the smallest members of the bear family. It is sometimes called the "Andean bear."

The spectacled bear is the only bear native to South America. It lives in forests high in the Andes Mountains.

This bear has black fur and whitish rings around its eyes that look like glasses, or spectacles.

These bears eat mostly fruit, berries, cacti, leaves and honey. They sometimes eat mice, rabbits and birds.

Spectacled bears are very good climbers. They build platforms in trees where they eat and sleep.

Spectacled bears are active mostly at night.

Because they
eat mostly plants,
these **bears** have very
strong jaws and wide,
flat teeth.

These bears are **shy.** They don't like to get **close to** people.

Spectacled bears are **endangered.** Fewer than 3000 of them are left in the wild.

Because they live in such **remote** areas, we don't know very much about **spectacled bears.**

Giant pandas are found in the mountains in **China**. They live in cool, wet **bamboo** forests.

Pandas like to sit on the ground and eat, but they are **good tree climbers**, too. They also **swim** well.

Pandas do not hibernate.

Pandas have wide, **flat back teeth** that **crush** bamboo leaves and **stems.**

Giant pandas only eat the leaves and shoots of bamboo. They spend 10 to 16 hours a day looking for food or **eating.**

Pandas have a special **wrist bone** that acts like a thumb. They use it to hold the bamboo **stalks.**

Giant pandas are **very rare** and **endangered.** Only about **1600 are left** in the wild.

These bears are very **timid.** They live in areas that are far **away from people.**

Female pandas have only **one cub** at a time. The cub **stays** with its **mother** for up to **two years**.

Asiatic Black Bear

The Asiatic black bear is also called "**moon bear.**"

Asiatic black bears **live in** Russia, China, India, Japan, Korea, Malaysia and **other parts of Asia.**

The Asiatic black bear is usually black with **big ears** and a whitish "V" on its chest. It also has a **mane of long hair** around its face.

Asiatic black bears spend about half their time in trees. That is more than any other bear.

Asiatic black bears live in thick forests on hills and **mountains.** They live in some of the same areas as giant pandas and even **eat bamboo**, the panda's favourite food.

These bears **will eat almost anything.** They like nuts, berries, insects, **fruit and honey.** They sometimes **eat meat.**

Sometimes these bears **hibernate.** That is **unusual** for bears that **live in Asia.**

Asiatic black bears like to walk on their **hind legs.** They can walk upright for **half a kilometre.**

Their paws **do not have fur.** That **helps** them climb trees.

Asiatic black bears sometimes attack humans.

Sloth Bear

Sloth bears **live in forests** and also on **grasslands** with boulders and shrubs for **shelter.** These bears are active **mostly at night.**

Sloth bears live in **India and Sri Lanka.** They have **shaggy,** black fur, long claws and a whitish "V" or "Y" on their **chest.**

The sloth bear often **carries its cubs on its back.**

The sloth bear **climbs** trees and knocks down **honeycombs** to eat. That is how it got its nickname **"honey bear."**

These bears like fruit, but they eat mostly ants, **beetles** and termites. They **use their lips** like a vacuum to **suck insects** from their nests.

Sloth bears **will run away** if they **hear or smell** people.

Sun bears live in forests. They sleep on **platforms** high above the ground **in trees.**

Sun bears get their name from the golden or white **patch on** their chest. It looks like the rising sun.

The sun bear is the **smallest** member of the **bear family.** It lives in **Southeast Asia.**

Sun Bear

This bear is also called "dog bear" because of its small size, short snout and small, round ears. Its short, smooth fur helps keep it cool.

Sun bears like honey. Their **long tongue** lets them eat honey from **beehives**.

The sun bear uses its **long claws** to rip open **trees** and **termite nests**.

Sun bears are **active** mostly at night. They **walk** through the forest looking for fruits, **berries**, insects, **small birds**, lizards **and mice**.

The Publisher: KidsWorld Books

Library and Archives Canada Cataloguing in Publication

Bears / Einstein Sisters.

ISBN 978-0-9938401-4-2 (pbk.)

1. Bears—Juvenile literature. I. Einstein Sisters, author

QL737.C27B39 2014   j599.78   C2014-903890-9

Cover Images: Front cover: grizzly and cub, davidrasmus / Thinkstock. *Back cover:* polar bear, JohnPitcher / Thinkstock; panda, amepl1 / Thinkstock; black bear cub, Geoff Kuchera / Thinkstock.

Background Graphics: abstract swirl, hakkiarslan / Thinkstock, 5, 9, 14, 21, 22, 26, 30, 37, 40, 48, 50, 54, 60; abstract background, Maryna Borsevych / Thinkstock, 7, 19, 32, 46, 63; pixels, Misko Kordic / Thinkstock, 2, 12, 16, 24, 28, 39, 42, 53, 57, 58.

Photo Credits: Steve Wilson / Flickr, 41. From Thinkstock: Alessandro Rizzolli, 43; ampys, 12; Angela Joyce, 24; Anup Shah, 56, 60; badins, 62–63; bergsbo, 22–23; camacho9999, 38; davidrasmus, 10, 26–27; Denise Kappa, 59; Dgwildlife, 11, 14–15; Dieter Meyrl, 6–7; EdwardVisserPhotography, 25; EEl_Tony, 32–33; elovodchenko, 8; Eric Gevaert, 57; foto76, 53; Fuse, 44, 46; Geoff Kuchera, 9; Glenn Nagel, 29, 34; gnagel, 58; hose_bw, 54; Hung_Chung_Chih, 45; JohnPitcher, 36–37; jonmccormackphoto, 18–19, 20, 21; Luiz Fernando&Souza Fernandes, 40; Lynn Bystrom, 13; Martina Berg, 61; mb-fotos, 62; Musat, 39, 42; nelik, 48; OST, 4–5; OSTILL, 50–51; Pete Nielsen, 49; Ron Sandford, 16; Sablin, 52; seread, 31; sorincolac, 3; Strekoza2, 2; stuckreed, 28; Tom Brakefield, 17; topten22photo, 51; webguzs, 30; Xiaoni Tong, 46–47; yotrak, 55; zanskar, 35; zizar2002, 26.

We acknowledge the financial support of the Government of Canada through the Canada Book Fund (CBF) for our publishing activities.

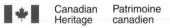

Canadian   Patrimoine
Heritage   canadien

PC: 27